Reseller Inventory log book

Personal Details

Name: ....

Adress: ....

Email: ....

Phone number: ....

WEEK OF _____

GOALS

1	2	3

MONDAY	TUESDAY	WEDNESDAY	THURSDAY

FRIDAY	SATURDAY	SUNDAY	NOTES

	MONDAY	TUESDAY	WEDNESDAY	THURSDAY	FRIDAY	SATURDAY	SUNDAY	TOTAL
LISTED								
SALES								

WEEK OF _____

GOALS

1   2   3

MONDAY	TUESDAY	WEDNESDAY	THURSDAY

FRIDAY	SATURDAY	SUNDAY	NOTES

	MONDAY	TUESDAY	WEDNESDAY	THURSDAY	FRIDAY	SATURDAY	SUNDAY	TOTAL
LISTED								
SALES								

WEEK OF _____ GOALS

1	2	3

MONDAY	TUESDAY	WEDNESDAY	THURSDAY

FRIDAY	SATURDAY	SUNDAY	NOTES

	MONDAY	TUESDAY	WEDNESDAY	THURSDAY	FRIDAY	SATURDAY	SUNDAY	TOTAL
LISTED								
SALES								

WEEK OF _____   GOALS

1   2   3

MONDAY	TUESDAY	WEDNESDAY	THURSDAY

FRIDAY	SATURDAY	SUNDAY	NOTES

	MONDAY	TUESDAY	WEDNESDAY	THURSDAY	FRIDAY	SATURDAY	SUNDAY	TOTAL
LISTED								
SALES								

WEEK OF _____

GOALS

1   2   3

MONDAY	TUESDAY	WEDNESDAY	THURSDAY

FRIDAY	SATURDAY	SUNDAY	NOTES

	MONDAY	TUESDAY	WEDNESDAY	THURSDAY	FRIDAY	SATURDAY	SUNDAY	TOTAL
LISTED								
SALES								

WEEK OF _____ GOALS

1   2   3

MONDAY	TUESDAY	WEDNESDAY	THURSDAY

FRIDAY	SATURDAY	SUNDAY	NOTES

	MONDAY	TUESDAY	WEDNESDAY	THURSDAY	FRIDAY	SATURDAY	SUNDAY	TOTAL
LISTED								
SALES								

WEEK OF _____

GOALS

1	2	3

MONDAY	TUESDAY	WEDNESDAY	THURSDAY

FRIDAY	SATURDAY	SUNDAY	NOTES

	MONDAY	TUESDAY	WEDNESDAY	THURSDAY	FRIDAY	SATURDAY	SUNDAY	TOTAL
LISTED								
SALES								

WEEK OF _____

GOALS

1	2	3

MONDAY	TUESDAY	WEDNESDAY	THURSDAY

FRIDAY	SATURDAY	SUNDAY	NOTES

	MONDAY	TUESDAY	WEDNESDAY	THURSDAY	FRIDAY	SATURDAY	SUNDAY	TOTAL
LISTED								
SALES								

WEEK OF _____

GOALS

1	2	3

MONDAY	TUESDAY	WEDNESDAY	THURSDAY

FRIDAY	SATURDAY	SUNDAY	NOTES

	MONDAY	TUESDAY	WEDNESDAY	THURSDAY	FRIDAY	SATURDAY	SUNDAY	TOTAL
LISTED								
SALES								

WEEK OF _____

GOALS

1	2	3

MONDAY	TUESDAY	WEDNESDAY	THURSDAY

FRIDAY	SATURDAY	SUNDAY	NOTES

	MONDAY	TUESDAY	WEDNESDAY	THURSDAY	FRIDAY	SATURDAY	SUNDAY	TOTAL
LISTED								
SALES								

WEEK OF _____

GOALS

1

2

3

MONDAY	TUESDAY	WEDNESDAY	THURSDAY

FRIDAY	SATURDAY	SUNDAY	NOTES

	MONDAY	TUESDAY	WEDNESDAY	THURSDAY	FRIDAY	SATURDAY	SUNDAY	TOTAL
LISTED								
SALES								

WEEK OF _____ GOALS

1 | 2 | 3

| MONDAY | TUESDAY | WEDNESDAY | THURSDAY |

| FRIDAY | SATURDAY | SUNDAY | NOTES |

	MONDAY	TUESDAY	WEDNESDAY	THURSDAY	FRIDAY	SATURDAY	SUNDAY	TOTAL
LISTED								
SALES								

WEEK OF _____

GOALS

1	2	3

MONDAY	TUESDAY	WEDNESDAY	THURSDAY

FRIDAY	SATURDAY	SUNDAY	NOTES

	MONDAY	TUESDAY	WEDNESDAY	THURSDAY	FRIDAY	SATURDAY	SUNDAY	TOTAL
LISTED								
SALES								

WEEK OF _____

GOALS

1

2

3

MONDAY	TUESDAY	WEDNESDAY	THURSDAY

FRIDAY	SATURDAY	SUNDAY	NOTES

	MONDAY	TUESDAY	WEDNESDAY	THURSDAY	FRIDAY	SATURDAY	SUNDAY	TOTAL
LISTED								
SALES								

WEEK OF _____ GOALS

1   2   3

MONDAY	TUESDAY	WEDNESDAY	THURSDAY

FRIDAY	SATURDAY	SUNDAY	NOTES

	MONDAY	TUESDAY	WEDNESDAY	THURSDAY	FRIDAY	SATURDAY	SUNDAY	TOTAL
LISTED								
SALES								

WEEK OF _____   GOALS

1	2	3

MONDAY	TUESDAY	WEDNESDAY	THURSDAY

FRIDAY	SATURDAY	SUNDAY	NOTES

	MONDAY	TUESDAY	WEDNESDAY	THURSDAY	FRIDAY	SATURDAY	SUNDAY	TOTAL
LISTED								
SALES								

WEEK OF _____ GOALS

1	2	3

MONDAY	TUESDAY	WEDNESDAY	THURSDAY

FRIDAY	SATURDAY	SUNDAY	NOTES

	MONDAY	TUESDAY	WEDNESDAY	THURSDAY	FRIDAY	SATURDAY	SUNDAY	TOTAL
LISTED								
SALES								

WEEK OF _____

GOALS

1	2	3

MONDAY	TUESDAY	WEDNESDAY	THURSDAY

FRIDAY	SATURDAY	SUNDAY	NOTES

	MONDAY	TUESDAY	WEDNESDAY	THURSDAY	FRIDAY	SATURDAY	SUNDAY	TOTAL
LISTED								
SALES								

WEEK OF _____

GOALS

1

2

3

MONDAY	TUESDAY	WEDNESDAY	THURSDAY

FRIDAY	SATURDAY	SUNDAY	NOTES

	MONDAY	TUESDAY	WEDNESDAY	THURSDAY	FRIDAY	SATURDAY	SUNDAY	TOTAL
LISTED								
SALES								

WEEK OF _____ GOALS

1	2	3

MONDAY	TUESDAY	WEDNESDAY	THURSDAY

FRIDAY	SATURDAY	SUNDAY	NOTES

	MONDAY	TUESDAY	WEDNESDAY	THURSDAY	FRIDAY	SATURDAY	SUNDAY	TOTAL
LISTED								
SALES								

WEEK OF _____ GOALS

1	2	3

MONDAY	TUESDAY	WEDNESDAY	THURSDAY

FRIDAY	SATURDAY	SUNDAY	NOTES

	MONDAY	TUESDAY	WEDNESDAY	THURSDAY	FRIDAY	SATURDAY	SUNDAY	TOTAL
LISTED								
SALES								

WEEK OF _____

GOALS

1 | 2 | 3

MONDAY	TUESDAY	WEDNESDAY	THURSDAY

FRIDAY	SATURDAY	SUNDAY	NOTES

	MONDAY	TUESDAY	WEDNESDAY	THURSDAY	FRIDAY	SATURDAY	SUNDAY	TOTAL
LISTED								
SALES								

WEEK OF _____

GOALS

1

2

3

	MONDAY	TUESDAY	WEDNESDAY	THURSDAY

	FRIDAY	SATURDAY	SUNDAY	NOTES

	MONDAY	TUESDAY	WEDNESDAY	THURSDAY	FRIDAY	SATURDAY	SUNDAY	TOTAL
LISTED								
SALES								

WEEK OF _____

GOALS

1	2	3

MONDAY	TUESDAY	WEDNESDAY	THURSDAY

FRIDAY	SATURDAY	SUNDAY	NOTES

	MONDAY	TUESDAY	WEDNESDAY	THURSDAY	FRIDAY	SATURDAY	SUNDAY	TOTAL
LISTED								
SALES								

WEEK OF _____

GOALS

1	2	3

MONDAY	TUESDAY	WEDNESDAY	THURSDAY

FRIDAY	SATURDAY	SUNDAY	NOTES

	MONDAY	TUESDAY	WEDNESDAY	THURSDAY	FRIDAY	SATURDAY	SUNDAY	TOTAL
LISTED								
SALES								

WEEK OF _____ GOALS

1 | 2 | 3

MONDAY	TUESDAY	WEDNESDAY	THURSDAY

FRIDAY	SATURDAY	SUNDAY	NOTES

	MONDAY	TUESDAY	WEDNESDAY	THURSDAY	FRIDAY	SATURDAY	SUNDAY	TOTAL
LISTED								
SALES								

WEEK OF _____

GOALS

1 | 2 | 3

MONDAY	TUESDAY	WEDNESDAY	THURSDAY

FRIDAY	SATURDAY	SUNDAY	NOTES

	MONDAY	TUESDAY	WEDNESDAY	THURSDAY	FRIDAY	SATURDAY	SUNDAY	TOTAL
LISTED								
SALES								

WEEK OF _____   GOALS

1	2	3

MONDAY	TUESDAY	WEDNESDAY	THURSDAY

FRIDAY	SATURDAY	SUNDAY	NOTES

	MONDAY	TUESDAY	WEDNESDAY	THURSDAY	FRIDAY	SATURDAY	SUNDAY	TOTAL
LISTED								
SALES								

WEEK OF _____

GOALS

1	2	3

MONDAY	TUESDAY	WEDNESDAY	THURSDAY

FRIDAY	SATURDAY	SUNDAY	NOTES

	MONDAY	TUESDAY	WEDNESDAY	THURSDAY	FRIDAY	SATURDAY	SUNDAY	TOTAL
LISTED								
SALES								

WEEK OF _____ GOALS

1 | 2 | 3

| MONDAY | TUESDAY | WEDNESDAY | THURSDAY |

| FRIDAY | SATURDAY | SUNDAY | NOTES |

	MONDAY	TUESDAY	WEDNESDAY	THURSDAY	FRIDAY	SATURDAY	SUNDAY	TOTAL
LISTED								
SALES								

WEEK OF _____

GOALS

1

2

3

MONDAY	TUESDAY	WEDNESDAY	THURSDAY

FRIDAY	SATURDAY	SUNDAY	NOTES

	MONDAY	TUESDAY	WEDNESDAY	THURSDAY	FRIDAY	SATURDAY	SUNDAY	TOTAL
LISTED								
SALES								

WEEK OF _____ GOALS

1 | 2 | 3

| MONDAY | TUESDAY | WEDNESDAY | THURSDAY |

| FRIDAY | SATURDAY | SUNDAY | NOTES |

	MONDAY	TUESDAY	WEDNESDAY	THURSDAY	FRIDAY	SATURDAY	SUNDAY	TOTAL
LISTED								
SALES								

WEEK OF _____ GOALS

1	2	3

MONDAY	TUESDAY	WEDNESDAY	THURSDAY

FRIDAY	SATURDAY	SUNDAY	NOTES

	MONDAY	TUESDAY	WEDNESDAY	THURSDAY	FRIDAY	SATURDAY	SUNDAY	TOTAL
LISTED								
SALES								

WEEK OF _____

GOALS

1 | 2 | 3

MONDAY	TUESDAY	WEDNESDAY	THURSDAY

FRIDAY	SATURDAY	SUNDAY	NOTES

	MONDAY	TUESDAY	WEDNESDAY	THURSDAY	FRIDAY	SATURDAY	SUNDAY	TOTAL
LISTED								
SALES								

WEEK OF _____

GOALS

1	2	3

MONDAY	TUESDAY	WEDNESDAY	THURSDAY

FRIDAY	SATURDAY	SUNDAY	NOTES

	MONDAY	TUESDAY	WEDNESDAY	THURSDAY	FRIDAY	SATURDAY	SUNDAY	TOTAL
LISTED								
SALES								

WEEK OF _____

GOALS

1	2	3

MONDAY	TUESDAY	WEDNESDAY	THURSDAY

FRIDAY	SATURDAY	SUNDAY	NOTES

	MONDAY	TUESDAY	WEDNESDAY	THURSDAY	FRIDAY	SATURDAY	SUNDAY	TOTAL
LISTED								
SALES								

WEEK OF _____ GOALS

1	2	3

MONDAY	TUESDAY	WEDNESDAY	THURSDAY

FRIDAY	SATURDAY	SUNDAY	NOTES

	MONDAY	TUESDAY	WEDNESDAY	THURSDAY	FRIDAY	SATURDAY	SUNDAY	TOTAL
LISTED								
SALES								

WEEK OF _____

GOALS

1

2

3

MONDAY	TUESDAY	WEDNESDAY	THURSDAY

FRIDAY	SATURDAY	SUNDAY	NOTES

	MONDAY	TUESDAY	WEDNESDAY	THURSDAY	FRIDAY	SATURDAY	SUNDAY	TOTAL
LISTED								
SALES								

WEEK OF _____

GOALS

1

2

3

MONDAY	TUESDAY	WEDNESDAY	THURSDAY

FRIDAY	SATURDAY	SUNDAY	NOTES

	MONDAY	TUESDAY	WEDNESDAY	THURSDAY	FRIDAY	SATURDAY	SUNDAY	TOTAL
LISTED								
SALES								

WEEK OF _____

GOALS

1 | 2 | 3

MONDAY	TUESDAY	WEDNESDAY	THURSDAY

FRIDAY	SATURDAY	SUNDAY	NOTES

	MONDAY	TUESDAY	WEDNESDAY	THURSDAY	FRIDAY	SATURDAY	SUNDAY	TOTAL
LISTED								
SALES								

WEEK OF _____

GOALS

1	2	3

MONDAY	TUESDAY	WEDNESDAY	THURSDAY

FRIDAY	SATURDAY	SUNDAY	NOTES

	MONDAY	TUESDAY	WEDNESDAY	THURSDAY	FRIDAY	SATURDAY	SUNDAY	TOTAL
LISTED								
SALES								

WEEK OF _____

GOALS

1

2

3

MONDAY	TUESDAY	WEDNESDAY	THURSDAY

FRIDAY	SATURDAY	SUNDAY	NOTES

	MONDAY	TUESDAY	WEDNESDAY	THURSDAY	FRIDAY	SATURDAY	SUNDAY	TOTAL
LISTED								
SALES								

WEEK OF _____ GOALS

1	2	3

MONDAY	TUESDAY	WEDNESDAY	THURSDAY

FRIDAY	SATURDAY	SUNDAY	NOTES

	MONDAY	TUESDAY	WEDNESDAY	THURSDAY	FRIDAY	SATURDAY	SUNDAY	TOTAL
LISTED								
SALES								

WEEK OF _____

GOALS

1   2   3

MONDAY	TUESDAY	WEDNESDAY	THURSDAY

FRIDAY	SATURDAY	SUNDAY	NOTES

	MONDAY	TUESDAY	WEDNESDAY	THURSDAY	FRIDAY	SATURDAY	SUNDAY	TOTAL
LISTED								
SALES								

WEEK OF _____

GOALS

1

2

3

MONDAY	TUESDAY	WEDNESDAY	THURSDAY

FRIDAY	SATURDAY	SUNDAY	NOTES

	MONDAY	TUESDAY	WEDNESDAY	THURSDAY	FRIDAY	SATURDAY	SUNDAY	TOTAL
LISTED								
SALES								

WEEK OF _____ GOALS

1   2   3

MONDAY	TUESDAY	WEDNESDAY	THURSDAY

FRIDAY	SATURDAY	SUNDAY	NOTES

	MONDAY	TUESDAY	WEDNESDAY	THURSDAY	FRIDAY	SATURDAY	SUNDAY	TOTAL
LISTED								
SALES								

WEEK OF _____

GOALS

1	2	3

MONDAY	TUESDAY	WEDNESDAY	THURSDAY

FRIDAY	SATURDAY	SUNDAY	NOTES

	MONDAY	TUESDAY	WEDNESDAY	THURSDAY	FRIDAY	SATURDAY	SUNDAY	TOTAL
LISTED								
SALES								

WEEK OF _____ GOALS

1	2	3

MONDAY	TUESDAY	WEDNESDAY	THURSDAY

FRIDAY	SATURDAY	SUNDAY	NOTES

	MONDAY	TUESDAY	WEDNESDAY	THURSDAY	FRIDAY	SATURDAY	SUNDAY	TOTAL
LISTED								
SALES								

WEEK OF _____

GOALS

1 | 2 | 3

MONDAY	TUESDAY	WEDNESDAY	THURSDAY

FRIDAY	SATURDAY	SUNDAY	NOTES

	MONDAY	TUESDAY	WEDNESDAY	THURSDAY	FRIDAY	SATURDAY	SUNDAY	TOTAL
LISTED								
SALES								

WEEK OF _____ GOALS

1 | 2 | 3

MONDAY	TUESDAY	WEDNESDAY	THURSDAY

FRIDAY	SATURDAY	SUNDAY	NOTES

	MONDAY	TUESDAY	WEDNESDAY	THURSDAY	FRIDAY	SATURDAY	SUNDAY	TOTAL
LISTED								
SALES								

WEEK OF _____

GOALS

1	2	3

MONDAY	TUESDAY	WEDNESDAY	THURSDAY

FRIDAY	SATURDAY	SUNDAY	NOTES

	MONDAY	TUESDAY	WEDNESDAY	THURSDAY	FRIDAY	SATURDAY	SUNDAY	TOTAL
LISTED								
SALES								

WEEK OF _____ GOALS

| 1 | 2 | 3 |

MONDAY	TUESDAY	WEDNESDAY	THURSDAY

FRIDAY	SATURDAY	SUNDAY	NOTES

	MONDAY	TUESDAY	WEDNESDAY	THURSDAY	FRIDAY	SATURDAY	SUNDAY	TOTAL
LISTED								
SALES								

WEEK OF _____

GOALS

1   2   3

MONDAY	TUESDAY	WEDNESDAY	THURSDAY
FRIDAY	SATURDAY	SUNDAY	NOTES

	MONDAY	TUESDAY	WEDNESDAY	THURSDAY	FRIDAY	SATURDAY	SUNDAY	TOTAL
LISTED								
SALES								

WEEK OF _____ GOALS

1   2   3

MONDAY	TUESDAY	WEDNESDAY	THURSDAY

FRIDAY	SATURDAY	SUNDAY	NOTES

	MONDAY	TUESDAY	WEDNESDAY	THURSDAY	FRIDAY	SATURDAY	SUNDAY	TOTAL
ISTED								
ALES								

WEEK OF _____ GOALS

1	2	3

MONDAY	TUESDAY	WEDNESDAY	THURSDAY

FRIDAY	SATURDAY	SUNDAY	NOTES

	MONDAY	TUESDAY	WEDNESDAY	THURSDAY	FRIDAY	SATURDAY	SUNDAY	TOTAL
LISTED								
SALES								

WEEK OF _____

GOALS

1	2	3

MONDAY	TUESDAY	WEDNESDAY	THURSDAY

FRIDAY	SATURDAY	SUNDAY	NOTES

	MONDAY	TUESDAY	WEDNESDAY	THURSDAY	FRIDAY	SATURDAY	SUNDAY	TOTAL
LISTED								
SALES								

WEEK OF _____

GOALS

1	2	3

MONDAY	TUESDAY	WEDNESDAY	THURSDAY

FRIDAY	SATURDAY	SUNDAY	NOTES

	MONDAY	TUESDAY	WEDNESDAY	THURSDAY	FRIDAY	SATURDAY	SUNDAY	TOTAL
LISTED								
SALES								

WEEK OF _____

GOALS

1

2

3

| MONDAY | TUESDAY | WEDNESDAY | THURSDAY |

| FRIDAY | SATURDAY | SUNDAY | NOTES |

	MONDAY	TUESDAY	WEDNESDAY	THURSDAY	FRIDAY	SATURDAY	SUNDAY	TOTAL
LISTED								
SALES								

WEEK OF _____

GOALS

1	2	3

MONDAY	TUESDAY	WEDNESDAY	THURSDAY

FRIDAY	SATURDAY	SUNDAY	NOTES

	MONDAY	TUESDAY	WEDNESDAY	THURSDAY	FRIDAY	SATURDAY	SUNDAY	TOTAL
LISTED								
SALES								

WEEK OF _____

GOALS

1	2	3

MONDAY	TUESDAY	WEDNESDAY	THURSDAY

FRIDAY	SATURDAY	SUNDAY	NOTES

	MONDAY	TUESDAY	WEDNESDAY	THURSDAY	FRIDAY	SATURDAY	SUNDAY	TOTAL
LISTED								
SALES								

WEEK OF _____ GOALS

1	2	3

MONDAY	TUESDAY	WEDNESDAY	THURSDAY

FRIDAY	SATURDAY	SUNDAY	NOTES

	MONDAY	TUESDAY	WEDNESDAY	THURSDAY	FRIDAY	SATURDAY	SUNDAY	TOTAL
LISTED								
SALES								

WEEK OF _____ GOALS

| 1 | 2 | 3 |

MONDAY	TUESDAY	WEDNESDAY	THURSDAY

FRIDAY	SATURDAY	SUNDAY	NOTES

	MONDAY	TUESDAY	WEDNESDAY	THURSDAY	FRIDAY	SATURDAY	SUNDAY	TOTAL
LISTED								
SALES								

WEEK OF _____

GOALS

1

2

3

MONDAY	TUESDAY	WEDNESDAY	THURSDAY

FRIDAY	SATURDAY	SUNDAY	NOTES

	MONDAY	TUESDAY	WEDNESDAY	THURSDAY	FRIDAY	SATURDAY	SUNDAY	TOTAL
LISTED								
SALES								

WEEK OF _____

GOALS

1

2

3

| MONDAY | TUESDAY | WEDNESDAY | THURSDAY |

| FRIDAY | SATURDAY | SUNDAY | NOTES |

	MONDAY	TUESDAY	WEDNESDAY	THURSDAY	FRIDAY	SATURDAY	SUNDAY	TOTAL
LISTED								
SALES								

WEEK OF _____

GOALS

1	2	3

MONDAY	TUESDAY	WEDNESDAY	THURSDAY

FRIDAY	SATURDAY	SUNDAY	NOTES

	MONDAY	TUESDAY	WEDNESDAY	THURSDAY	FRIDAY	SATURDAY	SUNDAY	TOTAL
LISTED								
SALES								

WEEK OF _____

GOALS

1 | 2 | 3

| MONDAY | TUESDAY | WEDNESDAY | THURSDAY |
| | | | |

| FRIDAY | SATURDAY | SUNDAY | NOTES |
| | | | |

	MONDAY	TUESDAY	WEDNESDAY	THURSDAY	FRIDAY	SATURDAY	SUNDAY	TOTAL
LISTED								
SALES								

WEEK OF _____

GOALS

1

2

3

MONDAY	TUESDAY	WEDNESDAY	THURSDAY

FRIDAY	SATURDAY	SUNDAY	NOTES

	MONDAY	TUESDAY	WEDNESDAY	THURSDAY	FRIDAY	SATURDAY	SUNDAY	TOTAL
LISTED								
SALES								

WEEK OF _____ GOALS

1 | 2 | 3

| MONDAY | TUESDAY | WEDNESDAY | THURSDAY |

| FRIDAY | SATURDAY | SUNDAY | NOTES |

	MONDAY	TUESDAY	WEDNESDAY	THURSDAY	FRIDAY	SATURDAY	SUNDAY	TOTAL
LISTED								
SALES								

WEEK OF _____

GOALS

1

2

3

MONDAY	TUESDAY	WEDNESDAY	THURSDAY

FRIDAY	SATURDAY	SUNDAY	NOTES

	MONDAY	TUESDAY	WEDNESDAY	THURSDAY	FRIDAY	SATURDAY	SUNDAY	TOTAL
LISTED								
SALES								

WEEK OF _____ GOALS

1	2	3

MONDAY	TUESDAY	WEDNESDAY	THURSDAY

FRIDAY	SATURDAY	SUNDAY	NOTES

	MONDAY	TUESDAY	WEDNESDAY	THURSDAY	FRIDAY	SATURDAY	SUNDAY	TOTAL
LISTED								
SALES								

WEEK OF _____

GOALS

1   2   3

MONDAY	TUESDAY	WEDNESDAY	THURSDAY

FRIDAY	SATURDAY	SUNDAY	NOTES

	MONDAY	TUESDAY	WEDNESDAY	THURSDAY	FRIDAY	SATURDAY	SUNDAY	TOTAL
LISTED								
SALES								

WEEK OF _____ GOALS

1 | 2 | 3

MONDAY	TUESDAY	WEDNESDAY	THURSDAY

FRIDAY	SATURDAY	SUNDAY	NOTES

	MONDAY	TUESDAY	WEDNESDAY	THURSDAY	FRIDAY	SATURDAY	SUNDAY	TOTAL
LISTED								
SALES								

WEEK OF _____

GOALS

1   2   3

MONDAY	TUESDAY	WEDNESDAY	THURSDAY

FRIDAY	SATURDAY	SUNDAY	NOTES

	MONDAY	TUESDAY	WEDNESDAY	THURSDAY	FRIDAY	SATURDAY	SUNDAY	TOTAL
LISTED								
SALES								

WEEK OF _____

GOALS

1

2

3

| MONDAY | TUESDAY | WEDNESDAY | THURSDAY |

| FRIDAY | SATURDAY | SUNDAY | NOTES |

	MONDAY	TUESDAY	WEDNESDAY	THURSDAY	FRIDAY	SATURDAY	SUNDAY	TOTAL
LISTED								
SALES								

WEEK OF _____

GOALS

1	2	3

MONDAY	TUESDAY	WEDNESDAY	THURSDAY

FRIDAY	SATURDAY	SUNDAY	NOTES

	MONDAY	TUESDAY	WEDNESDAY	THURSDAY	FRIDAY	SATURDAY	SUNDAY	TOTAL
LISTED								
SALES								

WEEK OF _____

GOALS

1	2	3

MONDAY	TUESDAY	WEDNESDAY	THURSDAY

FRIDAY	SATURDAY	SUNDAY	NOTES

	MONDAY	TUESDAY	WEDNESDAY	THURSDAY	FRIDAY	SATURDAY	SUNDAY	TOTAL
LISTED								
SALES								

WEEK OF _____

GOALS

1

2

3

	MONDAY	TUESDAY	WEDNESDAY	THURSDAY

	FRIDAY	SATURDAY	SUNDAY	NOTES

	MONDAY	TUESDAY	WEDNESDAY	THURSDAY	FRIDAY	SATURDAY	SUNDAY	TOTAL
LISTED								
SALES								

WEEK OF _____   GOALS

1   2   3

MONDAY	TUESDAY	WEDNESDAY	THURSDAY

FRIDAY	SATURDAY	SUNDAY	NOTES

	MONDAY	TUESDAY	WEDNESDAY	THURSDAY	FRIDAY	SATURDAY	SUNDAY	TOTAL
LISTED								
SALES								

WEEK OF _____

GOALS

1	2	3

MONDAY	TUESDAY	WEDNESDAY	THURSDAY

FRIDAY	SATURDAY	SUNDAY	NOTES

	MONDAY	TUESDAY	WEDNESDAY	THURSDAY	FRIDAY	SATURDAY	SUNDAY	TOTAL
LISTED								
SALES								

WEEK OF _____

GOALS

1   2   3

MONDAY	TUESDAY	WEDNESDAY	THURSDAY

FRIDAY	SATURDAY	SUNDAY	NOTES

	MONDAY	TUESDAY	WEDNESDAY	THURSDAY	FRIDAY	SATURDAY	SUNDAY	TOTAL
LISTED								
SALES								

WEEK OF _____

GOALS

1	2	3

MONDAY	TUESDAY	WEDNESDAY	THURSDAY
FRIDAY	SATURDAY	SUNDAY	NOTES

	MONDAY	TUESDAY	WEDNESDAY	THURSDAY	FRIDAY	SATURDAY	SUNDAY	TOTAL
LISTED								
SALES								

WEEK OF _____ GOALS

1   2   3

| MONDAY | TUESDAY | WEDNESDAY | THURSDAY |

| FRIDAY | SATURDAY | SUNDAY | NOTES |

	MONDAY	TUESDAY	WEDNESDAY	THURSDAY	FRIDAY	SATURDAY	SUNDAY	TOTAL
LISTED								
SALES								

WEEK OF _____ GOALS

1	2	3

MONDAY	TUESDAY	WEDNESDAY	THURSDAY

FRIDAY	SATURDAY	SUNDAY	NOTES

	MONDAY	TUESDAY	WEDNESDAY	THURSDAY	FRIDAY	SATURDAY	SUNDAY	TOTAL
LISTED								
SALES								

WEEK OF _____   GOALS

1	2	3

MONDAY	TUESDAY	WEDNESDAY	THURSDAY

FRIDAY	SATURDAY	SUNDAY	NOTES

	MONDAY	TUESDAY	WEDNESDAY	THURSDAY	FRIDAY	SATURDAY	SUNDAY	TOTAL
LISTED								
SALES								

WEEK OF _____   GOALS

1	2	3

MONDAY	TUESDAY	WEDNESDAY	THURSDAY

FRIDAY	SATURDAY	SUNDAY	NOTES

	MONDAY	TUESDAY	WEDNESDAY	THURSDAY	FRIDAY	SATURDAY	SUNDAY	TOTAL
LISTED								
SALES								

WEEK OF _____ GOALS

1	2	3

MONDAY	TUESDAY	WEDNESDAY	THURSDAY

FRIDAY	SATURDAY	SUNDAY	NOTES

	MONDAY	TUESDAY	WEDNESDAY	THURSDAY	FRIDAY	SATURDAY	SUNDAY	TOTAL
ISTED								
SALES								

WEEK OF _____

GOALS

1

2

3

MONDAY	TUESDAY	WEDNESDAY	THURSDAY
FRIDAY	SATURDAY	SUNDAY	NOTES

	MONDAY	TUESDAY	WEDNESDAY	THURSDAY	FRIDAY	SATURDAY	SUNDAY	TOTAL
LISTED								
SALES								

WEEK OF _____

GOALS

1

2

3

	MONDAY	TUESDAY	WEDNESDAY	THURSDAY

	FRIDAY	SATURDAY	SUNDAY	NOTES

	MONDAY	TUESDAY	WEDNESDAY	THURSDAY	FRIDAY	SATURDAY	SUNDAY	TOTAL
LISTED								
SALES								

WEEK OF _____

GOALS

1

2

3

MONDAY	TUESDAY	WEDNESDAY	THURSDAY

FRIDAY	SATURDAY	SUNDAY	NOTES

	MONDAY	TUESDAY	WEDNESDAY	THURSDAY	FRIDAY	SATURDAY	SUNDAY	TOTAL
LISTED								
SALES								

WEEK OF _____

GOALS

1	2	3

MONDAY	TUESDAY	WEDNESDAY	THURSDAY

FRIDAY	SATURDAY	SUNDAY	NOTES

	MONDAY	TUESDAY	WEDNESDAY	THURSDAY	FRIDAY	SATURDAY	SUNDAY	TOTAL
LISTED								
SALES								

WEEK OF _____ GOALS

1	2	3

MONDAY	TUESDAY	WEDNESDAY	THURSDAY

FRIDAY	SATURDAY	SUNDAY	NOTES

	MONDAY	TUESDAY	WEDNESDAY	THURSDAY	FRIDAY	SATURDAY	SUNDAY	TOTAL
LISTED								
SALES								

WEEK OF _____

GOALS

1 | | 2 | | 3 |

MONDAY	TUESDAY	WEDNESDAY	THURSDAY

FRIDAY	SATURDAY	SUNDAY	NOTES

	MONDAY	TUESDAY	WEDNESDAY	THURSDAY	FRIDAY	SATURDAY	SUNDAY	TOTAL
LISTED								
SALES								

WEEK OF _____

GOALS

1	2	3

MONDAY	TUESDAY	WEDNESDAY	THURSDAY

FRIDAY	SATURDAY	SUNDAY	NOTES

	MONDAY	TUESDAY	WEDNESDAY	THURSDAY	FRIDAY	SATURDAY	SUNDAY	TOTAL
LISTED								
SALES								

WEEK OF _____   GOALS

1   2   3

| MONDAY | TUESDAY | WEDNESDAY | THURSDAY |

| FRIDAY | SATURDAY | SUNDAY | NOTES |

	MONDAY	TUESDAY	WEDNESDAY	THURSDAY	FRIDAY	SATURDAY	SUNDAY	TOTAL
LISTED								
SALES								

WEEK OF _____

GOALS

1	2	3

MONDAY	TUESDAY	WEDNESDAY	THURSDAY

FRIDAY	SATURDAY	SUNDAY	NOTES

	MONDAY	TUESDAY	WEDNESDAY	THURSDAY	FRIDAY	SATURDAY	SUNDAY	TOTAL
LISTED								
SALES								

WEEK OF _____

GOALS

1

2

3

MONDAY	TUESDAY	WEDNESDAY	THURSDAY

FRIDAY	SATURDAY	SUNDAY	NOTES

	MONDAY	TUESDAY	WEDNESDAY	THURSDAY	FRIDAY	SATURDAY	SUNDAY	TOTAL
LISTED								
SALES								

WEEK OF _____

GOALS

| 1 | 2 | 3 |

| MONDAY | TUESDAY | WEDNESDAY | THURSDAY |

| FRIDAY | SATURDAY | SUNDAY | NOTES |

	MONDAY	TUESDAY	WEDNESDAY	THURSDAY	FRIDAY	SATURDAY	SUNDAY	TOTAL
LISTED								
SALES								

WEEK OF _____   GOALS

1   2   3

| MONDAY | TUESDAY | WEDNESDAY | THURSDAY |

| FRIDAY | SATURDAY | SUNDAY | NOTES |

	MONDAY	TUESDAY	WEDNESDAY	THURSDAY	FRIDAY	SATURDAY	SUNDAY	TOTAL
LISTED								
SALES								

WEEK OF _____ GOALS

1	2	3

MONDAY	TUESDAY	WEDNESDAY	THURSDAY

FRIDAY	SATURDAY	SUNDAY	NOTES

	MONDAY	TUESDAY	WEDNESDAY	THURSDAY	FRIDAY	SATURDAY	SUNDAY	TOTAL
LISTED								
SALES								

WEEK OF _____ GOALS

1	2	3

MONDAY	TUESDAY	WEDNESDAY	THURSDAY

FRIDAY	SATURDAY	SUNDAY	NOTES

	MONDAY	TUESDAY	WEDNESDAY	THURSDAY	FRIDAY	SATURDAY	SUNDAY	TOTAL
LISTED								
SALES								

WEEK OF _____

GOALS

1 | 2 | 3

MONDAY	TUESDAY	WEDNESDAY	THURSDAY

FRIDAY	SATURDAY	SUNDAY	NOTES

	MONDAY	TUESDAY	WEDNESDAY	THURSDAY	FRIDAY	SATURDAY	SUNDAY	TOTAL
LISTED								
SALES								

WEEK OF _____

GOALS

1 | 2 | 3

| MONDAY | TUESDAY | WEDNESDAY | THURSDAY |

| FRIDAY | SATURDAY | SUNDAY | NOTES |

	MONDAY	TUESDAY	WEDNESDAY	THURSDAY	FRIDAY	SATURDAY	SUNDAY	TOTAL
LISTED								
SALES								

WEEK OF _____

GOALS

1	2	3

MONDAY	TUESDAY	WEDNESDAY	THURSDAY

FRIDAY	SATURDAY	SUNDAY	NOTES

	MONDAY	TUESDAY	WEDNESDAY	THURSDAY	FRIDAY	SATURDAY	SUNDAY	TOTAL
LISTED								
SALES								

WEEK OF _____

GOALS

1

2

3

MONDAY	TUESDAY	WEDNESDAY	THURSDAY

FRIDAY	SATURDAY	SUNDAY	NOTES

	MONDAY	TUESDAY	WEDNESDAY	THURSDAY	FRIDAY	SATURDAY	SUNDAY	TOTAL
LISTED								
SALES								

WEEK OF _____

GOALS

1	2	3

MONDAY	TUESDAY	WEDNESDAY	THURSDAY

FRIDAY	SATURDAY	SUNDAY	NOTES

	MONDAY	TUESDAY	WEDNESDAY	THURSDAY	FRIDAY	SATURDAY	SUNDAY	TOTAL
LISTED								
SALES								

WEEK OF _____ GOALS

| | 2 | | 3 |

| MONDAY | TUESDAY | WEDNESDAY | THURSDAY |

| FRIDAY | SATURDAY | SUNDAY | NOTES |

	MONDAY	TUESDAY	WEDNESDAY	THURSDAY	FRIDAY	SATURDAY	SUNDAY	TOTAL
LISTED								
SALES								

WEEK OF _____

GOALS

1	2	3

MONDAY	TUESDAY	WEDNESDAY	THURSDAY

FRIDAY	SATURDAY	SUNDAY	NOTES

	MONDAY	TUESDAY	WEDNESDAY	THURSDAY	FRIDAY	SATURDAY	SUNDAY	TOTAL
LISTED								
SALES								

WEEK OF _____ GOALS

1	2	3

MONDAY	TUESDAY	WEDNESDAY	THURSDAY

FRIDAY	SATURDAY	SUNDAY	NOTES

	MONDAY	TUESDAY	WEDNESDAY	THURSDAY	FRIDAY	SATURDAY	SUNDAY	TOTAL
LISTED								
SALES								

WEEK OF _____

GOALS

1	2	3

MONDAY	TUESDAY	WEDNESDAY	THURSDAY

FRIDAY	SATURDAY	SUNDAY	NOTES

	MONDAY	TUESDAY	WEDNESDAY	THURSDAY	FRIDAY	SATURDAY	SUNDAY	TOTAL
LISTED								
SALES								

WEEK OF _____ GOALS

1   2   3

MONDAY	TUESDAY	WEDNESDAY	THURSDAY

FRIDAY	SATURDAY	SUNDAY	NOTES

	MONDAY	TUESDAY	WEDNESDAY	THURSDAY	FRIDAY	SATURDAY	SUNDAY	TOTAL
LISTED								
SALES								

WEEK OF _____

GOALS

1

2

3

	MONDAY	TUESDAY	WEDNESDAY	THURSDAY

	FRIDAY	SATURDAY	SUNDAY	NOTES

	MONDAY	TUESDAY	WEDNESDAY	THURSDAY	FRIDAY	SATURDAY	SUNDAY	TOTAL
LISTED								
SALES								

WEEK OF _____ GOALS

1	2	3

MONDAY	TUESDAY	WEDNESDAY	THURSDAY

FRIDAY	SATURDAY	SUNDAY	NOTES

	MONDAY	TUESDAY	WEDNESDAY	THURSDAY	FRIDAY	SATURDAY	SUNDAY	TOTAL
LISTED								
SALES								

WEEK OF _____ GOALS

1	2	3

MONDAY	TUESDAY	WEDNESDAY	THURSDAY

FRIDAY	SATURDAY	SUNDAY	NOTES

	MONDAY	TUESDAY	WEDNESDAY	THURSDAY	FRIDAY	SATURDAY	SUNDAY	TOTAL
LISTED								
SALES								

WEEK OF _____ GOALS

1   2   3

MONDAY	TUESDAY	WEDNESDAY	THURSDAY

FRIDAY	SATURDAY	SUNDAY	NOTES

	MONDAY	TUESDAY	WEDNESDAY	THURSDAY	FRIDAY	SATURDAY	SUNDAY	TOTAL
LISTED								
SALES								

WEEK OF _____

GOALS

1

2

3

| | MONDAY | | | | TUESDAY | | | | WEDNESDAY | | | | THURSDAY |

| | FRIDAY | | | | SATURDAY | | | | SUNDAY | | | | NOTES |

	MONDAY	TUESDAY	WEDNESDAY	THURSDAY	FRIDAY	SATURDAY	SUNDAY	TOTAL
LISTED								
SALES								

WEEK OF _____ GOALS

1 | 2 | 3

| MONDAY | TUESDAY | WEDNESDAY | THURSDAY |

| FRIDAY | SATURDAY | SUNDAY | NOTES |

	MONDAY	TUESDAY	WEDNESDAY	THURSDAY	FRIDAY	SATURDAY	SUNDAY	TOTAL
LISTED								
SALES								

WEEK OF _____ GOALS

1 | 2 | 3

MONDAY	TUESDAY	WEDNESDAY	THURSDAY

FRIDAY	SATURDAY	SUNDAY	NOTES

	MONDAY	TUESDAY	WEDNESDAY	THURSDAY	FRIDAY	SATURDAY	SUNDAY	TOTAL
LISTED								
SALES								

WEEK OF _____

GOALS

1   2   3

MONDAY	TUESDAY	WEDNESDAY	THURSDAY

FRIDAY	SATURDAY	SUNDAY	NOTES

	MONDAY	TUESDAY	WEDNESDAY	THURSDAY	FRIDAY	SATURDAY	SUNDAY	TOTAL
_ISTED								
SALES								

WEEK OF _____

GOALS

1

2

3

MONDAY	TUESDAY	WEDNESDAY	THURSDAY

FRIDAY	SATURDAY	SUNDAY	NOTES

	MONDAY	TUESDAY	WEDNESDAY	THURSDAY	FRIDAY	SATURDAY	SUNDAY	TOTAL
LISTED								
SALES								

Printed in Great Britain
by Amazon

40253799R00071